WRITE SOURCE

Inside Writing

RESEARCH REPORTS

TE

. . . a self-contained student writing unit,
complete with instruction, guidelines,
activities, and writing space

WRITE SOURCE®

GREAT SOURCE EDUCATION GROUP

a division of Houghton Mifflin Company
Wilmington, Massachusetts

www.greatsource.com

Consulting Educators

We want to offer a special thanks to urban curriculum coordinator Dr. Mildred Pearson and to the entire Write Source/Great Source team for all their help. In addition, *Inside Writing* is a reality because of the help and advice of the following educators:

Linda Albertson	Rhoda Goodwin	Elhadji Ndaw	Yolanda Tynes
Amita Antao	Marguerite Guy	Trinette Patterson	Jackie Veith
Lisa Ariens	Jerry Hajewski	Regina Peña	Larry Vernor
Connie Blair	Mark Harris	Colleen Rourke	Agnes V. Williams
Robert Day	Shirley Minga	Mora Snowden	Gail Winograd
Pauline Eadie	Rhoda Nathan	Seth Sondag	

Field-Test Reviewers

Theodis Adams
Jackson Main
   Elementary School
Hempstead, New York

Jaimie Cogua
Jackson Academy
Omaha, Nebraska

Lori Cross
Mechanicsville
   Elementary School
Mechanicsville, Virginia

Juanita Diggins
Liberty Elementary School
Tucson, Arizona

Michele Ferentinos
Cornelia F. Bradford No. 16E
Jersey City, New Jersey

Lori Guyant
Samuel Clemens
   Elementary School
Milwaukee, Wisconsin

Ivy Hagedorn
McKinstry Elementary School
Waterloo, Iowa

Vincenzo LaRuina
Gardiner Manor
   Elementary School
Bay Shore, New York

Kowanda Lee
Washington Elementary School
Rockford, Illinois

Patrick Mooney
Holy Rosary School
Woodland, California

Pam Myrick
Rock Springs
   Elementary School
Apopka, Florida

Nia Nicole Nicholas
Westport Academy #225
Baltimore City, Maryland

Candace Queeney
Joseph Medill Primary School
Chicago, Illinois

Robert Savant
Junipero Serra School
San Francisco, California

Linda Siverson-Hall
Interdistrict Downtown School
Minneapolis, Minnesota

Authors

Dave Kemper and Pat Sebranek

Printed in the United States of America

International Standard Book Number: 0-669-50376-2 (teacher's edition)

1 2 3 4 5 6 7 8 9 10 -BA- 10 09 08 07 06 05 04 03

Planning Notes:
Research Reports

Unit Overview:

Research Reports

As with all *Inside Writing* units, the report writing unit is ready to put in the hands of your students. Within this booklet they will find step-by-step directions, graphic organizers, and appealing examples to help them with their work.

In this unit, students are asked to write a research report about a landmark in the United States. The unit assignments instruct students to choose a topic, research it, organize their data, and write the report. An optional activity introduces students to the process of writing a bibliography. The unit includes a sample report for students to use as a model for their writing.

Rationale

- In the "Universe of Discourse," report writing is an important form of expository writing requiring students to collect information from multiple sources.
- Writing a report can help students develop higher-level thinking skills (understanding, compiling, analyzing).
- Learning how to write reports is important in the academic world and in the workplace.

Major Concepts

- A report must go through a series of steps—planning, writing, revising, and editing and proofreading—before it is ready to be published.
- Questions are the basis for research.
- Taking notes helps to track research.
- Citing sources adds credibility to a report.
- Assessment is part of the writing process.

Strategies and Skills That Students Will Practice

- Selecting a subject
- Identifying potential sources
- Learning to cite sources

- Brainstorming questions for research
- Using note cards and a fact sheet
- Outlining
- Writing the beginning, middle, and ending parts of a report
- Learning to write effective topic sentences
- Using transitions between paragraphs
- Varying sentence beginnings
- Capitalizing names of people and things
- Creating a bibliography
- Evaluating reports using a rubric

Performance Standards

Students are expected to . . .

- select relevant subjects.
- use prewriting strategies to generate and organize ideas.
- support main ideas with facts and details.
- revise and edit their writing, striving for completeness, personal voice, specific word choice, smooth-reading sentences, and correctness.

Reinforcing Skills

- Students can use the *Writers Express* or *All Write* handbook for additional instructions related to writing research reports. (See page 18TE for handbook correlations.)
- Editing and proofreading skills can be reinforced and expanded by implementing exercises from *Inside Writing Skills* available for each level. (See page 9TE for suggestions.)

Weekly Planning Chart

The weekly planning chart should be viewed only as a suggested schedule. Adjust accordingly to fit your weekly lesson plans. Your students may need extra time to complete some of the assignments.

Weekly Planning Chart

Day	WEEK ONE	Pages	Skills
1	**Understanding the Unit** Reviewing the Unit Basics	inside front cover, 1-3	*understanding research reports and the assignment*
	Completing a Warm-Up Activity	4	*identifying famous landmarks*
2	**Working with a Sample Report** Reading and Reacting to a Sample Report	5-8	*discussing the report's content; using a rubric to assess*
3	**Prewriting** Selecting a Topic	10-11	*choosing a landmark to write about*
	Identifying Sources	12	*learning about kinds of sources*
	Optional: Recording Sources	13	*listing sources*
	Writing Fact-Finding Questions	14	*brainstorming questions*
4	**Prewriting** Researching Your Report	15-17	*using note cards and a fact sheet to collect information*
5	**Prewriting** Outlining Your Report	18-19	*completing a sentence outline*

Day	WEEK TWO	Pages	Skills
1	**Prewriting** Knowing the Parts of a Report	20	*learning how reports work*
	Writing Starting Your Report	22	*writing an effective beginning*
2	**Writing** Developing the Middle Paragraphs	23-25	*adding details and facts*
3	**Writing** Ending Your Report	26	*creating an effective ending*
4	**Writing** Forming a Complete First Draft	26	*completing the first draft*
5	**Revising** Skills Activity: Reviewing Topic Sentences	28	*developing good topic sentences*
	Skills Activity: Using Transitions Between Paragraphs	29	*tying paragraphs together*
	Optional: Sharing Assessed Models	12TE-14TE	*evaluating student writing*
	Peer Responding	30	*using a peer-response sheet*

Weekly Planning Chart

Day	WEEK THREE	Pages	Skills
1	**Revising** Skills Activity: Revising in Action	31	*learning how to revise*
	Using a Checklist	32	*reviewing and revising first drafts*
	Skills Activity: Adding a Title	33	*creating a title*
2	**Revising** Writing a Complete Revised Draft	34	*completing the revised writing*
3	**Editing and Proofreading** Skills Activity: Editing for Style	36	*making sentence beginnings different*
	Skills Activity: Editing for Correctness	37	*capitalizing names of people and things*
4	**Editing and Proofreading** Editing in Action	38-39	*learning how to edit*
	Optional: Creating a Bibliography	40	*compiling a bibliography*
	Using a Checklist	41	*checking for style and correctness*
	Writing the Final Copy	42-46	*completing the report*
5	**Publishing** Sharing Final Copies	8	*using a rubric to evaluate*

Daily Lesson Plans: Week One

DAY 1

Understanding the Unit

Reviewing the Unit Basics

- Discuss "About the Unit" (inside front cover). Remind students that they will share their finished reports with their classmates.
- Review the table of contents and "Assignment Checklist: Research Reports" (pages 1-2). Students can use the checklist to keep track of their assignments and due dates.
- Read and discuss page 3. Tell students that reports share information. Explain that a report is about one specific topic (in this unit, a landmark). A report is made up of interesting and important factual information found in reliable sources, like encyclopedias, books, magazines, and so on. Lead a classroom discussion about famous landmarks (natural and man-made) in this country.

Completing a Report Writing Warm-Up Activity

- Implement "What Is It? Where Is It?" (page 4). This activity will put students in a frame of mind to think about landmarks. You may wish to bring in photos of other landmarks in the United States for students to identify.
- *Optional:* Implement the "Prereading Activity" (page 11TE) in which students think about landmarks in their city and state.

DAY 2

Working with a Sample Report

Reading a Sample Report

- Have students read the sample report (pages 5-6), or read it aloud to the class. (If you wish, point out the female gender reference that is used when referring to a ship.) Ask students to pay close attention to the side notes, which identify the main parts of the report. Review the parts before implementing page 7.

Reacting to the Reading

- Implement "Reacting to the Reading" (page 7). Students may look at the sample report on pages 5-6 if they don't know the answer to a question. Invite students to share with the class their answers to the last question.

- *Optional:* Using "Important Stylistic Features" (page 11TE) as a guide, discuss two stylistic features—details and creativity—in the model report.

- As a class, assess the sample using the rubric on page 8. First analyze the *ideas* by deciding if the writing contains specific details and if it holds the reader's attention. Then go on to *organization, voice,* and so on. You may want to limit the assessment to one or two of the traits on the rubric. Inform students that this rubric will be used to assess their own reports.

 ESL TIP ESL students will benefit from a patient explanation of just what a research report is. Tell them that a research report shares interesting information. Looking for information is research, and sharing information is reporting.

DAY 3

Prewriting

Selecting a Topic

- Implement "Choosing Your Landmark" (pages 10-11). Begin by having students review the list of landmarks. If you did not brainstorm and list landmarks found in your state and city as a prereading activity, you may want to do that now. Post the list in your writing center. Ask students where they might find information about the landmarks. In this activity, students are asked to choose landmarks that sound interesting to them. Then they generate questions to guide their research. Remind them that they should choose a subject that truly interests them; otherwise, they may find it hard to write an effective report. (Help students choose landmarks that will be easy to research.)

Identifying Sources

- Tell students what types of research materials you want them to use for their reports. Then review page 12 with the class.

- *Optional:* Implement "Recording Sources" (page 13), which illustrates for students how to list sources.

Writing Fact-Finding Questions

- Implement "Writing Fact-Finding Questions" (page 14) in which students brainstorm questions they want to research for their reports. Review the strategy of using the 5 W and H questions. Upon completion of this page, students should choose the three most important questions.

ESL students may find it difficult to choose the three most important questions. A class discussion about the 5 W's and H may help them decide which questions to choose.

DAY 4

Prewriting

Researching Your Report

- Implement "Collecting Your Details" (pages 15-16) and "Listing Other Interesting Facts" (page 17). First model the note-card process on page 15. (You may wish to make a poster for students to refer to.) Also review the example facts on page 17. Allow ample time for students to complete their research. It is important that you carefully monitor the fact-finding process. If you have assigned bibliographies, remind your students to list the source along with the facts and details on each note card.

ESL students may find doing research difficult. Consider pairing an ESL student with a native-speaking classmate and having them conduct their research together.

DAY 5

Prewriting

Outlining Your Report

- Review "Making an Outline" (pages 18-19) with the class. Have students compare the sample note card on page 15 with the information under Roman numeral I on page 18. Ask student volunteers to model the beginning of an outline using their Roman numeral I cards. Make sure that students clearly understand the outlining process using the questions and facts on their note cards before they complete their sentence outlines. Closely monitor this activity. *Note:* Tell students that they may not need all of the subcategories (A., B., C., D.). However, they should fill in at least two details under each main point.

Daily Lesson Plans: Week Two

DAY 1

Prewriting

Knowing the Parts of a Report

- Review page 20 with the class. Discuss the three main parts of a report. Point out the linking words and phrases at the bottom of the page. These will help students connect the ideas, sentences, and paragraphs in their writing.

Writing

Starting Your Report

- *Optional:* Consider implementing "Reviewing Topic Sentences" page 28. Save the "Next Step" for later.
- Implement "Starting Your Report" (page 22). Read aloud to the class the sample on page 22 and the first paragraph of the report on pages 5-6. Discuss the methods these writers used to catch the reader's interest. Have students identify the topic of the sample on page 22. Remind them that their fact sheets (page 17) may help them find ideas for this part of the report.

 ESL TIP Using Niagara Falls, model the four suggestions for capturing the reader's interest. Start with an anecdote: "Imagine you are in a tiny boat below a roaring waterfall. . . . " Or share an interesting fact: "Every minute, 34 million gallons of water pour over Niagara Falls." Begin with a surprising idea: "Niagara Falls is one Great Lake pouring into another." Or start with a question: "Did you know that one day, Niagara Falls ran dry?"

DAY 2

Writing

Developing the Middle Paragraphs

- Implement "Developing the Middle Paragraphs" (pages 23-25). Begin by reading and discussing the sample paragraph on page 23. Have students identify the main idea and supporting details. Review the middle paragraphs in the sample on pages 5-6. Tell students that their reports will also have three middle paragraphs. Each one will tell something interesting or important about the landmark. (Remind students that the information for this part will come from their outlines on pages 18-19.)

DAY 3

Writing

Ending Your Report

- Implement "Ending Your Report" (page 26). Have students review the ending paragraphs on pages 26 and 6. Remind them to review page 17 for ideas to end their reports. After this writing session, ask volunteers to share their endings with the class. (Save the "Next Step" for tomorrow.)

DAY 4

Writing

Forming a Complete First Draft

- Assign the "Next Step" on page 26. Students should write a complete copy of their first drafts on their own paper. Instruct them to write on every other line to make the revising process easier. Students should feel free to add new words and ideas, and to make notes about things they want to change. Remind them to store their drafts in the back pocket of the booklet.

DAY 5

Revising

Skills Activities

- Implement "Reviewing Topic Sentences" (page 28). If you used this activity earlier, simply assign the "Next Step" now.
- Discuss "Using Transitions Between Paragraphs" (page 29) and have students complete the activity.

Sharing Assessed Models

- *Optional:* Share the assessed student reports (12TE-14TE) to help students evaluate the effectiveness of their writing. (Make copies of the reports or display them on an overhead projector.)

Peer Responding

- Have students react to each other's writing by implementing "Getting a Second Opinion" (page 30).

Be sure to pair ESL students with supportive peers for this activity. Emphasize the importance of interesting ideas rather than mechanical correctness.

Daily Lesson Plans: Week Three

DAY 1

Revising

Skills Activity: Revising in Action

- Review "Revising in Action" (page 31). Remind students that revising is a standard step in the writing process. Discuss the revisions made in the example and assign the exercise at the bottom of the page.

Using a Checklist to Revise

- Have students revise their first drafts using "Checking Your Progress" (page 32). Emphasize that revising is the process of improving the ideas, organization, and voice in writing. Checking for spelling, punctuation, and grammar should wait.

Skills Activity: Adding a Title

- Implement "Adding a Title" (page 33). Discuss "Title Tips" before having students complete the exercise at the bottom of the page.

DAY 2

Revising

Writing a Complete Revised Draft

- Review the revising tips on page 34. Then have students write a complete revised draft on their own paper.

DAY 3

Editing and Proofreading

Skills Activity: Editing for Style

- Implement "Making Sentence Beginnings Different" (page 36). Discuss the examples at the top of the page, and then assign the exercises. Ask volunteers to share their rewritten sentences with the class.

Skills Activity: Editing for Correctness

- Implement "Capitalizing Names of People and Things" (page 37). Review the basic capitalization rules with the class, and assign the exercises at the bottom of the page. Check them together in class.

Inside Writing Skills activities to consider:

Capital Letters (pages 27-34)

Plurals (pages 35-38)

Compound Subjects and Verbs (pages 81-82)

ESL TIP

Consider pairing students for the capitalization activity. Different languages have different capitalization rules, and ESL students may benefit from the help of native-language speakers.

DAY 4

Editing and Proofreading

Editing in Action

• Review "Editing and Proofreading Symbols" (page 38) and "Editing in Action" (page 39). Have students complete the proofreading exercise at the bottom of page 39. If possible, provide colored pens for this exercise.

Using a Checklist to Edit and Proofread

• *Optional:* Implement "Creating a Bibliography" (page 40). Review the example with students and revisit the information on page 13. Remind students that a bibliography includes the sources they used in writing their reports.

• Have students edit their revised writing following "Checking Your Progress" (page 41). In addition to self-editing, have the students pair up to edit each other's work.

Writing the Final Copy

• Review the writing tips on page 42; then provide time for students to write and proofread their final copies (pages 43-46). Assign a final due date.

DAY 5

Publishing

Sharing Final Copies

• Have student volunteers share their final drafts. Classmates should offer one positive comment about each report.

 Pair up reluctant students to share their reports with each other, or have them conference with you.

Formal Assessment Note: For a more traditional approach, guide students through a self-evaluation of their writing using the rubric on page 8. You may choose to use the 5-point scale used for evaluating the writing samples on pages 12TE-15TE or a point system established by your district.

About the Sample Report

The sample model on pages 5-6 reports about a landmark that many children will find interesting—the oldest commissioned battleship in the world, the U.S.S. *Constitution*. The report includes interesting facts and details about the construction of the ship and its most famous voyages, including the one that coined the ship's nickname, Old Ironsides.

Prereading Activity

Have students imagine that someone from another country is coming to visit them for one week. Their mission is to create a plan that includes visits to the landmarks in their city and state. Have students tell where they would take their visitor and why.

Vocabulary

rigged Outfitted, equipped

afloat In the water, at sea

hull Frame, or body, of a ship

outfight Fight harder than

Important Stylistic Features

DETAILS AND AUDIENCE: Details and facts should fit the audience. As students research, remind them to watch for facts and details that their classmates might enjoy. In the model report, the author picks up interesting information about the construction of the ship. (It is very different from today's ships.) She also tells about travels that would be of interest to her classmates (sailing the West Indies, fighting pirates in the Mediterranean, battling at sea). Encourage your students to use facts and details that interest them. Remind them to help readers hear, see, smell, taste, and feel the subject.

BE CREATIVE: Challenge students to think of their subjects from a new or creative perspective. In the model, the writer first sees the battleship as an out-of-place object in the landscape. Have students think about what the times were like when their landmarks were first constructed or discovered. What makes these landmarks stand out? What made them famous? Thinking of landmarks in a specific historical context can help students write creatively.

Assessed Writing Samples

Pages 12TE-15TE include three sample reports assessed using the rubric on page 8. Use these samples to help students with their writing and revising. (See Week Two, DAY 5, in "Daily Lesson Plans," page 8TE.) You may also use the samples as a guide when you evaluate your students' final copies. A 5-point scale is used to evaluate these samples, but the rubric will work with any point scale.

Report Writing Assessment

EXCELLENT

Hallidie's Folly

One of the most famous landmarks in America is in San Francisco, California. Would you believe that it is the cable cars? Did you know that they are the only national landmark that can move around?

There was a good reason for cable cars to be invented. In 1869, a man named Andrew Smith Hallidie saw a bad accident. In those days, horses pulled streetcars. One day, a streetcar pulled by horses fell backward down a steep San Francisco hill. That made Mr. Hallidie decide to invent a better way of getting around. In 1873, his cable cars started running.

The wood and steel cars are pulled by a thick wire rope under the tracks. The car moves when the driver squeezes a lever that grabs the moving rope. "Here we go!" calls the conductor. Cable cars go at about nine miles an hour. When they get to the end of the line, they have to turn around. A special place called a turnaround moves the cars to turn them back in the right direction.

9.7 million people ride 40 landmark cable cars every year. The cars can carry more than 60 people at a time. There once were 600 cable cars. There is also a cable car museum in San Francisco. That museum has the first cable car ever built.

In 1873, people called Mr. Hallidie's invention Hallidie's Folly. A folly is something that is foolish. What would those people say now if they saw this famous landmark is still in use more than 100 years later?

Bibliography

"Cable Cars." <u>The World Book Encyclopedia</u>. 2000 ed.

Clarkson, Richard. "Hallidie's Folly." <u>California Travel Life</u> 30 June
    2002: 22-23.

Williamson, James. <u>Cable Cars</u>. San Francisco: Special Places Press,
    1999.

Report Writing Rubric

<u>5</u> **Stimulating Ideas**
- The writing contains specific details about the topic.
- The writing holds the reader's interest from start to finish.

<u>5</u> **Logical Organization**
- The writing includes a clear beginning, middle, and ending.
- The writing presents facts, figures, and examples in an easy-to-follow way.
- The middle paragraphs are organized according to time or importance.

<u>5</u> **Personal Voice**
- The writing shows that the writer cares about the subject.
- The writing has an honest and interested voice.

<u>5</u> **Well-Chosen Words**
- The writing uses specific nouns and verbs.
- The writing includes linking words and phrases.

<u>5</u> **Smooth Sentences**
- The writing flows from one sentence to the next.
- The sentences are clear and easy to read.

<u>4</u> **Correct, Accurate Copy**
- The writing follows the basic rules of grammar, spelling, and punctuation.
- The writing uses the form suggested by the teacher.

1 Incomplete   **2** Poor   **3** Fair   **4** Good   **5** Excellent

COMMENTS:
What an interesting topic! I enjoyed reading your report. You did a good job of organizing your information. Remember to spell out a number when it begins a sentence. Nice work.

The Rocks Have Faces

Many landmarks are rocks. But not many rocks have faces. One very important one does. It is called Mount Rushmore.

Mount Rushmore has four faces. George Wahsington, Jefferson Thomas, Thomas Roosevelt, and Abe Lincoln. These men were presidents of the United States. That is why they have faces on a rock. Wahsington has a head as big as a man 465 feet tall. That is a very big man.

The faces are fake because they are made by men. They used dinamite and drills to make the faces in the big rock. It happened long ago in 1927. The man who invented the heads is named Gutson Borgum who is now dead.

You can see Mount Rushmore when you take a vacation. It is in the mountains. The landmark is in the National Park Systim, And it is fun to see.

This is a very famus landmark. You should go there because these are the biggest heads you will ever see.

Bibliography

"Mount Rushmore National Memorial." The World Book Encyclopedia. 2000 ed.

Report Writing Rubric

3 Stimulating Ideas
- The writing contains specific details about the topic.
- The writing holds the reader's interest from start to finish.

3 Logical Organization
- The writing includes a clear beginning, middle, and ending.
- The writing presents facts, figures, and examples in an easy-to-follow way.
- The middle paragraphs are organized according to time or importance.

4 Personal Voice
- The writing shows that the writer cares about the subject.
- The writing has an honest and interested voice.

2 Well-Chosen Words
- The writing uses specific nouns and verbs.
- The writing includes linking words and phrases.

3 Smooth Sentences
- The writing flows from one sentence to the next.
- The sentences are clear and easy to read.

2 Correct, Accurate Copy
- The writing follows the basic rules of grammar, spelling, and punctuation.
- The writing uses the form suggested by the teacher.

1 Incomplete **2** Poor **3** Fair **4** Good **5** Excellent

COMMENTS:

The beginning of your report catches the reader's interest. Carefully check the names of the presidents carved on the mountain and the name of the designer. In what state and mountain range is Mount Rushmore? Be very careful to check your work before you hand it in. Try to find more than one source.

The Statue of Liberty

It is a landmark that is in New York city. Peeple like to clime up it and look at the water. Maybe you would to? You can do it if you go there. The statue is made in France a long time a go. They moved it to the USA then. Lots of peeple say that it means Freedum. It is very tall. You can clime up inside it. And look out of the head. That wood be so cool. You can see lots of stuff up there.

You can read about it in books. You can see it in movies. It is even on tv. Maybe you would like to go there some day. I would like to.

Bibliographies

Book about statue of liberty

Encyclopedia about statue of liberty

Report Writing Rubric

2 Stimulating Ideas
- The writing contains specific details about the topic.
- The writing holds the reader's interest from start to finish.

1 Logical Organization
- The writing includes a clear beginning, middle, and ending.
- The writing presents facts, figures, and examples in an easy-to-follow way.
- The middle paragraphs are organized according to time or importance.

3 Personal Voice
- The writing shows that the writer cares about the subject.
- The writing has an honest and interested voice.

2 Well-Chosen Words
- The writing uses specific nouns and verbs.
- The writing includes linking words and phrases.

2 Smooth Sentences
- The writing flows from one sentence to the next.
- The sentences are clear and easy to read.

1 Correct, Accurate Copy
- The writing follows the basic rules of grammar, spelling, and punctuation.
- The writing uses the form suggested by the teacher.

1 Incomplete **2** Poor **3** Fair **4** Good **5** Excellent

COMMENTS:

You certainly picked a very famous and interesting landmark. Now you need to add many more facts and details. Where in New York City can you find the statue? When was it made in France? Why was it made? Who brought it to the United States? How was it put together? Always use your dictionary to look up any words you aren't quite sure of.

Optional Activities for Multiple Intelligences

Consider implementing one or more of the following activities during the unit. (The intelligences addressed in each activity are listed in italics.)

✱ **Warm-Up** (page 4)
Create a travel poster for a landmark in the United States. Your poster should tell where it is and include one good reason for visiting it.
Spatial Intelligence

✱ **Reading a Sample Report** (pages 5-6)
Find out more about the history of the U.S.S. *Constitution* in the War of 1812. Give an oral report to the class about what you have learned.
Logical and Verbal Intelligences

✱ **Prewriting** (pages 10-11)
Interview an adult who has visited a famous landmark in this country to find out his or her thoughts and feelings about it. Report to the class about your interview.
Interpersonal and Verbal Intelligences

✱ **Writing** (pages 22-26)
Write a rap song about your landmark. Teach it to the class.
Interpersonal and Musical Intelligences

✱ **Revising** (page 33)
Imagine that you had the task of renaming the Statue of Liberty, the White House, and the Grand Canyon. What would you call them and why?
Logical Intelligence

Additional Report Writing Prompts

For additional writing practice, assign one or more of the following report writing prompts.

■ You have been asked to build a memorial to a person, a place, or a thing. Write a report telling what you would build and why.

■ Write a report about a famous landmark in a country other than the United States.

■ Write a report about a Native American landmark.

■ Write a report about a famous zoo in the United States.

■ An important event is sometimes called "a landmark event." Write a report about a landmark event in the history of the United States.

Cross-Curricular Thematic Unit

Science
Naturalist and Logical Intelligences
Mount St. Helens is a volcano and a national landmark. Write a report about how volcanoes are formed and why they erupt.

Language Arts
Linguistic and Verbal Intelligences
Write a letter to the caretakers at a national landmark. Ask for brochures and other information about the landmark. Make an oral report to the class when you receive a response.

Literature
Logical and Linguistic Intelligences
Find a nonfiction book about a state or city. Make sure the book includes photos of landmarks. Create a magazine ad that encourages your classmates to check out the book. Be sure to include the title of the book and the names of some of the interesting landmarks.

Physical Education
Bodily-Kinesthetic Intelligence
There are 70 flights of stairs in the Sears Tower, or 1,400 steps. Stand in place and pretend to climb to the top. Are you tired?

Theme: Landmarks

Art
Spatial Intelligence
Design a travel brochure for a landmark in your state. See if you can find or draw some pictures to include.

Music
Logical and Musical Intelligences
The Star-Spangled Banner Flag House is a landmark in Baltimore, Maryland. Find out why it is important. An important song is connected to this house. What is it? Perform it for the class.

Speech
Verbal and Logical Intelligences
Imagine that you are a tour guide for a state or local landmark. Write a script in which you tell visitors about the history of the landmark. Pretend that your classmates are visiting the landmark. Read your script to them.

Social Studies
Logical and Spatial Intelligences
Make a map of the Santa Fe National Historic Trail. Add landmarks that you will find along the way.

Correlations to Write Source Handbooks

Inside Writing **RESEARCH REPORTS**	*Writers Express* ©2000	*All Write* ©2003
3 Introduction: Research Reports	192	195
5 Reading and Reacting	202-203	196-197
8 Understanding Traits	18-23	17-22
PREWRITING: **Planning Your Writing**		
10 Selecting a Topic	36-39, 193	36-39
12 Finding Information	194, 259-263, 268	199, 230-231, 239-241
13 Recording Sources	201	206
14 Fact Finding with the 5 W's and H	45, 334	48, 132, 164
15 Collecting Details	194-196	199-201
17 Using a Fact Sheet	194-195	199-200
18 Outlining Your Information	49, 96, 197	96
20 Learning About the Structure	198-200, 202-203	91, 196-197, 202-203
WRITING: **Connecting Your Ideas**		
22 Starting Your Report	51, 90, 198	52, 93, 97, 202
23 Developing the Middle Paragraphs	52, 90, 199	53, 97, 203
26 Ending Your Report	53, 90, 200	53, 97, 203
26 Forming a Complete First Draft	50-53, 202-203	52-53, 196-197
REVISING: **Improving Your Writing**		
28 Reviewing Topic Sentences	77	79
29 Using Transitions Between Paragraphs	85	87, 88
30 Peer Responding	60-63	57-60
31 Revising in Action	15, 56, 58-59, 200	14, 55, 56, 204
32 Using a Checklist	23, 57	22, 55, 207
33 Adding a Title	59, 391	56, 363
34 Writing a Complete Revised Draft	56-59, 200	55-56, 204
EDITING: **Checking for Style and Correctness**		
36 Varying Sentence Beginnings	65	63
37 Capitalizing Names of People and Things	390-392	362-366
39 Editing in Action	16, 64-66	15, 63, 204
40 Creating a Bibliography	201, 203	206
41 Using a Checklist	23, 67	22, 62
42 Writing the Final Copy	26, 202-203	24-25

Inside Writing RESEARCH REPORTS

Assignment Checklist: **Research Reports**

This checklist will help you keep track of the assignments in this unit. Check the box next to each unit assignment as you complete it.

Due Date

_____ ☐ Research Report Warm-Up (page 4)
_____ ☐ Reacting to the Reading (page 7)

PREWRITING: Planning Your Writing

_____ ☐ Choosing Your Landmark (pages 10-11)
_____ ☐ Finding Information (page 12)
_____ ☐ Recording Sources (page 13)
_____ ☐ Writing Fact-Finding Questions (page 14)
_____ ☐ Collecting Your Details (pages 15-16)
_____ ☐ Listing Other Interesting Facts (page 17)
_____ ☐ Making an Outline (pages 18-19)

WRITING: Connecting Your Ideas

_____ ☐ Starting Your Report (page 22)
_____ ☐ Developing the Middle Paragraphs (pages 23-25)
_____ ☐ Ending Your Report (page 26)

REVISING: Improving Your Writing

_____ ☐ Reviewing Topic Sentences (page 28)
_____ ☐ Using Transitions Between Paragraphs (page 29)
_____ ☐ Getting a Second Opinion (page 30)
_____ ☐ Revising in Action (page 31)
_____ ☐ Checking Your Progress (page 32)
_____ ☐ Adding a Title (page 33)
_____ ☐ Writing a Complete Revised Draft (page 34)

EDITING: Checking for Style and Correctness

_____ ☐ Making Sentence Beginnings Different (page 36)
_____ ☐ Capitalizing Names of People and Things (page 37)
_____ ☐ Editing in Action (page 39)
_____ ☐ Creating a Bibliography (page 40)
_____ ☐ Checking Your Progress (page 41)
_____ ☐ Writing the Final Copy (pages 42-46)

"Writers are the main landmarks of the past."

— Edward G. Bulwer-Lytton,
English novelist
(1803-1873)

Research Reports

A landmark is a well-known place or thing in a country, state, or city. The Liberty Bell, the Grand Canyon, and the White House are landmarks. The Golden Gate Bridge, the Empire State Building, and the Indianapolis Motor Speedway are also popular landmarks. Your own city may have a landmark or two. Think about it. Is there a well-known place in your community or area—something that visitors always want to see?

In this unit, you will choose a landmark in the United States and write a report about it for your classmates. A report is a kind of writing that shares information. You will use books, magazines, and other sources to find facts and details about your landmark.

Date ....

Research Report Warm-Up: **What Is It? Where Is It?**

Directions | Do you recognize these landmarks? Write the name of each landmark and the state where it is located.

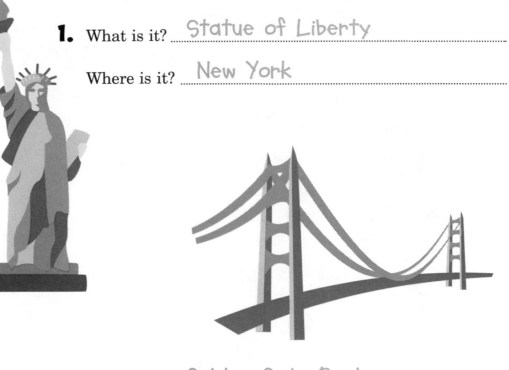

1. What is it? ..... Statue of Liberty ....

Where is it? ..... New York ....

2. What is it? ..... Golden Gate Bridge ....

Where is it? ..... California ....

3. What is it? ..... Mount Rushmore ....

Where is it? ..... South Dakota ....

Reading a Sample Report

Read this sample report about another famous landmark. Read the side notes, too. They tell you about the parts of a report.

Huzzah! It's Old Ironsides

Beginning
The writer gets the reader's attention and introduces the subject.

You are in an airplane flying over Boston, Massachusetts. You look out the window. Down below you see the ocean, a harbor, and an old wooden ship armed with cannons and **rigged** with sails! What is this place? It is the Charlestown Navy Yard. You are looking at the U.S.S. Constitution, the oldest warship **afloat** in the world.

Middle
The writer includes important and interesting facts and details.

The U.S.S. Constitution was built between 1794 and 1797. She was rigged with 36 sails, and the wood for her **hull** came from 2,000 trees. The cannons had copper parts made by Paul Revere. When she set sail in 1798, she was strong enough to **outfight** any ship her size.

Her first trip was to the West Indies. Two years later, she fought pirates in the Mediterranean Sea. In the War of 1812, against the British, she had her most famous battle. On August 19, 1812, she was firing cannonballs at a British ship. The ship shot

VOCABULARY

rigged Outfitted, equipped
afloat In the water, at sea
hull Frame, or body, of a ship
outfight Fight harder than

back and hit the U.S.S. <u>Constitution</u>. Someone saw the cannonball bounce off her 21-inch-thick wooden sides. He shouted, "Huzzah! Her sides are made of iron!" That is how she got her nickname, Old Ironsides.

Did you know that the U.S.S. <u>Constitution</u> is still a part of the U.S. Navy? Today, the U.S.S. <u>Constitution</u> is a famous American landmark. You can visit her at the Charlestown Navy Yard in Boston, Massachusetts. Sailors dressed in old-time costumes will take you through the ship. Along the way, you will hear stories of her battles. You will also see how the crew lived.

More than 400,000 people visit this famous American landmark every year. Along with the U.S.S. <u>Constitution</u> Museum right next to the ship, it is one of the most popular landmarks in Boston.

Ending
The writer sums up the main idea and leaves the reader with something to think about.

Reacting to the Reading

Directions   See how much you remember about Old Ironsides. Put an "X" by the correct answer. You may look back at the report on pages 5-6 to check your answers.

1. The topic of the report is

_____ **A.** Boston, Massachusetts.

_____ **B.** ships.

___X___ **C.** the U.S.S. Constitution.

2. In the report's first paragraph, the writer

_____ **A.** explains what a landmark is.

___X___ **B.** gets the reader's attention and introduces the subject.

_____ **C.** includes details about the ship's nickname.

3. The reader learns about the details of the ship's trips in

_____ **A.** the beginning of the report.

___X___ **B.** the middle of the report.

_____ **C.** the end of the report.

4. Which detail in this report interested you the most?

....

....

5. What else would you like to know about Old Ironsides? Write one question on the lines below.

....

....

Evaluating: **What Makes Report Writing Good?**

This rubric, or checklist, will help you know what to look for in a good research report. You can use this checklist to help you write your report and to help you evaluate, or judge, your finished writing.

Report Writing Rubric

___ Stimulating Ideas
- The writing contains specific details about the topic.
- The writing holds the reader's interest from start to finish.

___ Logical Organization
- The writing includes a clear beginning, middle, and ending.
- The writing presents facts, figures, and examples in an easy-to-follow way.
- The middle paragraphs are organized according to time or importance.

___ Personal Voice
- The writing shows that the writer cares about the subject.
- The writing has an honest and interested voice.

___ Well-Chosen Words
- The writing uses specific nouns and verbs.
- The writing includes linking words and phrases.

___ Smooth Sentences
- The writing flows from one sentence to the next.
- The sentences are clear and easy to read.

___ Correct, Accurate Copy
- The writing follows the basic rules of grammar, spelling, and punctuation.
- The writing uses the form suggested by the teacher.

Prewriting
Planning Your Writing

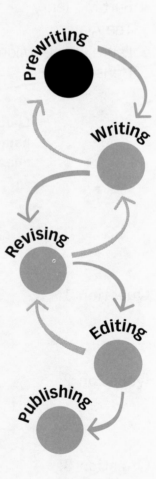

Prewriting

Writing

Revising

Editing

Publishing

Date ....

Prewriting Choosing Your Landmark

Now it's time to choose a landmark to write about. A landmark is a well-known place or thing, and there are thousands to choose from in the United States. Read through these examples:

- Mount Rushmore
- Grand Canyon
- Niagara Falls
- Hoover Dam
- Mount St. Helens
- Devils Tower
- Route 66
- Sears Tower
- Gateway Arch
- Space Needle
- Golden Gate Bridge
- Fort McHenry
- The Alamo
- Laura Ingalls Wilder's House

- Sacajawea State Park
- Harriet Tubman Home
- Wrigley Field
- Dry Tortugas
- Centennial Olympic Park
- Jefferson Memorial
- Lincoln Memorial
- Washington Monument
- Vietnam Veterans Memorial
- U.S. Capitol Building
- The White House
- Statue of Liberty
- Liberty Bell
- Williamsburg

Consider landmarks in your own city or state:

- Statues
- Lighthouses
- Indian burial grounds
- Historic neighborhoods
- Homes of famous people
- Historic buildings
- Sports stadiums
- Lakes, rivers, mountains
- Historic roads
- Forts and battle sites
- Bridges and tunnels

Directions **Choose three landmarks that you would like to learn about. Write their names in the boxes on this and the next page. Then write three questions that you would like to research about each landmark.**

Work Zone

Landmark: ....

Question 1: ....

....

Question 2: ....

....

Question 3: ....

....

Landmark: ....

Question 1: ....

....

Question 2: ....

....

Question 3: ....

....

Landmark: ....

Question 1: ....

....

Question 2: ....

....

Question 3: ....

....

Choose one of the three landmarks for your report. Write the name of your subject on the line below. Then have your teacher approve the idea.

My subject: ....

Date ....

Prewriting Finding Information

Now that you have an interesting subject (your landmark), you need to find true and interesting facts about it. Here are some places to look.

Books Books often give a lot of information on one subject. Some landmarks may have whole books written about them.

Magazines Magazines usually tell an interesting story and share facts about a specific place or subject. Travel and history magazines may have articles about your landmark.

Encyclopedias Encyclopedias tell you basic facts. This would be a good place to learn where a landmark is located and why it is important.

Internet The Internet can provide a great deal of information if you know how to search the Web. Your landmark might have its own Web page with additional links to other useful sites (information).

Interviews People are often your most valuable source of information. If you can't find information about a local landmark, try interviewing someone at your city library, historical museum, or historical society.

Your teacher will tell you which sources to use for your report. If you have trouble finding information, ask your teacher or librarian for help.

Directions Check the sources you plan to use for your report.

_____ **1.** Encyclopedias   _____ **4.** Internet

_____ **2.** Books   _____ **5.** Interviews with

_____ **3.** Magazines   _____

Work Zone

Prewriting Recording Sources

You may be asked to make a list of the sources for your report—a *bibliography*. This page shows how to record your sources.

BOOKS: Author (last name first). <u>Title</u> (underlined). City where the book is published: Publisher, copyright date.

> Dallas, George M. <u>The White House</u>. New York: Famous Homes Press, 1995.

Directions | In the space below, write a bibliography entry for this book:

Work Zone

> **Book title:** *Amazing Landmarks*
> **Author:** Anthony Marcus
> **City where book is published:** New York
> **Publisher:** Amazing Publishing
> **Copyright date:** 2003

Marcus, Anthony. <u>Amazing Landmarks</u>. New York: Amazing

Publishing, 2003.

Record other sources in the following ways:

MAGAZINES: Author (last name first). "Article title." <u>Title of the magazine</u> (underlined) date (day month year): Page numbers of the article.

> Hayek, Susan. "Welcome Home, Mr. President." <u>American Life</u> 2 May 2000: 8-9.

ENCYCLOPEDIAS: "Article title." <u>Title of the encyclopedia</u> (underlined). Edition or version (year).

> "White House." <u>The World Book Encyclopedia</u>. 2002 ed.

INTERNET: "Web page title." <u>Web site title</u> (underlined). <Electronic address>.

> "Life in the White House." <u>Welcome to the White House</u>. <http://whitehouse.gov>.

INTERVIEWS: Person interviewed (last name first). Type of interview. Date (day month year).

> Carter, James. Personal interview. 12 Dec. 2003.

Date ....

Prewriting Writing Fact-Finding Questions

Next, you will think of questions about your landmark.

Work Zone

Directions | Write the name of your landmark on the line below. Then turn on your brainpower. Write all the questions you can think of about your landmark. Number them 1, 2, 3, and so on. If you need more space, use your own paper. (Hint: Think about questions that begin with *who, what, when, where, why,* and *how.*)

Landmark: ....

....

....

....

....

....

....

....

....

....

....

....

Decide which three questions are most important to answer in your report. Number them with Roman numerals like this: I., II., III.

Prewriting Collecting Your Details

There are many ways to collect details for a report. In this unit, you will use note cards. As you research your topic, write facts on the cards, as in this example.

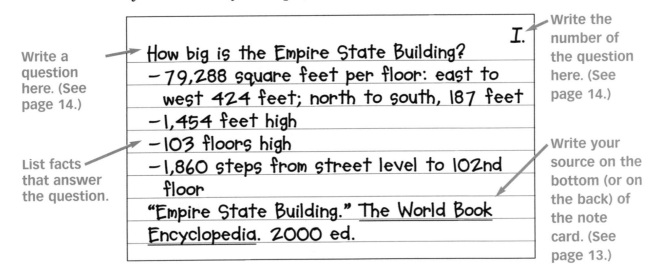

Write the number of the question here. (See page 14.)

Write a question here. (See page 14.)

List facts that answer the question.

I.

How big is the Empire State Building?
— 79,288 square feet per floor: east to west 424 feet; north to south, 187 feet
— 1,454 feet high
— 103 floors high
— 1,860 steps from street level to 102nd floor

"Empire State Building." The World Book Encyclopedia. 2000 ed.

Write your source on the bottom (or on the back) of the note card. (See page 13.)

Directions Use a separate card for each book, magazine, or other source you use. On each card, write one question, its number, and facts that answer the question. The blank cards on this and the next page will get you started. Make more on your own paper and store them in the back pocket of this booklet. (Before you begin, read page 17.)

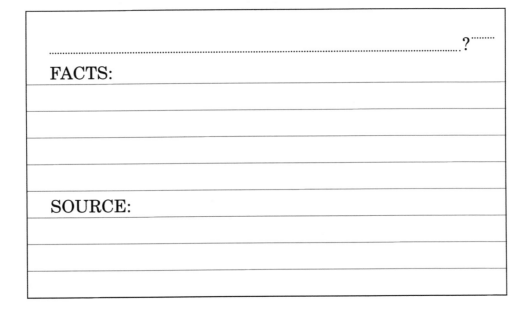

.... ?..........

FACTS:

SOURCE:

....
....?

FACTS:

SOURCE:

....
....?

FACTS:

SOURCE:

....
....?

FACTS:

SOURCE:

Date ....

Prewriting Listing Other Interesting Facts

As you search for information, you may find some interesting facts that don't answer any of your questions. List the facts and the source as shown below. Perhaps you could use one of them to begin or end your report.

Fact	Source
The Empire State Building gets struck by lightning about 100 times a year.	"Empire State Building." Official Internet Site. <http://empirestatebuilding.com>.

Directions

Use this organizer to keep track of interesting facts that don't fit your questions. If you need more space, use your own paper and put it in the back pocket of this booklet.

Fact	Source

Work Zone

Date ....

Prewriting Making an Outline

It's time to put your information in order. You can organize facts with a simple sentence outline like this one.

I. II. III.
Turn each of your three questions (I, II, III) into an interesting sentence.

I. The Empire State Building is one of the tallest buildings in the United States.
    A. It is 1,454 feet high.
    B. There are 103 floors.
    C. There are 1,860 steps from the street to the 102nd floor.
    D. It has 79,288 square feet per floor.

A. B. C. D.
Turn your facts into sentences, too.

II. Building the Empire State Building was a huge project.
    A. Building began March 17, 1930.
    B. The frame went up at a rate of 4-1/2 stories a week.
    C. Construction took one year and 45 days, seven days a week.
    D. It is made of 200,000 cubic feet of limestone and 210,000 square feet of marble.

III. The top of the Empire State Building is a popular place to visit.
    A. A fast elevator goes to the 86th floor.
    B. All of New York City can be seen from the viewing deck.
    C. Many famous people have been at the top, including princes, queens, and leaders from almost every country in the world.

Directions
Make a sentence outline for your report. First turn your three questions from the Next Step on page 14 (I., II., III.) into statements. Then do the same thing with the facts you found (pages 15-17).

Work Zone

I. ....

....

A. ....

....

B. ....

....

C. ....

....

II. ....

....

    A. ....

....

    B. ....

....

    C. ....

....

III. ....

....

    A. ....

....

    B. ....

....

    C. ....

....

Look at your outline. The sentences you wrote for I., II., and III. will become the main ideas for the middle paragraphs of your report. The sentences you wrote for A., B., C., and so on, will help to support those main ideas.

Prewriting Knowing the Parts of a Report

The next step is to write your report. It will have three parts: a beginning, a middle, and an ending. Each part has a special purpose. Look at the chart below to see the parts and how they fit together.

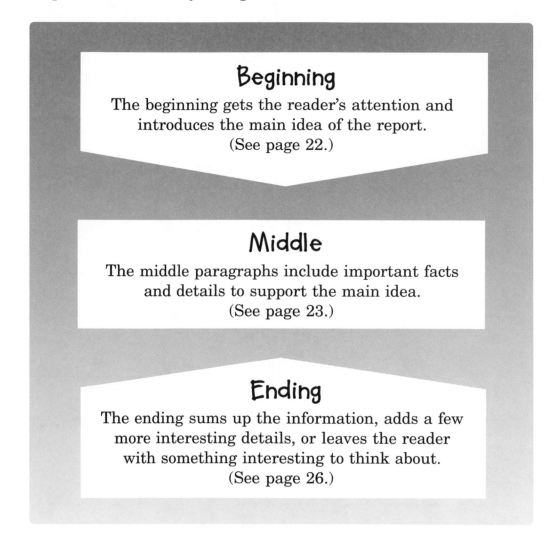

Beginning
The beginning gets the reader's attention and introduces the main idea of the report.
(See page 22.)

Middle
The middle paragraphs include important facts and details to support the main idea.
(See page 23.)

Ending
The ending sums up the information, adds a few more interesting details, or leaves the reader with something interesting to think about.
(See page 26.)

Linking Words and Phrases

You can use linking words and phrases to make the sentences in your report flow more smoothly. Here are some words and phrases for you to use.

again	**and**	**for instance**	**as well**
also	**besides**	**next**	**along with**
another	**for example**	**finally**	**in addition**

Writing
Connecting Your Ideas

Prewriting

Writing

Revising

Editing

Publishing

Date ....

Writing Starting Your Report

The first paragraph of your report introduces the subject (your landmark) and catches your reader's interest. The report on pages 5-6 begins with an *anecdote* (a little story) that leads the reader to the subject—the U.S.S. *Constitution*. The writer could also have started with an interesting fact, a surprising idea, or a question, as in this example:

My Report
Beginning
Middle
Ending

Would you like to visit Ramona Quimby? You can! She's in Portland, Oregon, at the Beverly Cleary Sculpture Garden for Children.

Directions Now, you try. Write the first paragraph of your report in the space below. Before you begin, check out the interesting facts you wrote on page 17. One of them might be perfect to use in this paragraph.

Work Zone

Date ....

Writing Developing the Middle Paragraphs

The middle of your report will have three paragraphs. Each one should share a main idea along with supporting details and facts. Read the middle paragraphs in the report on pages 5-6. Then read this one:

The Beverly Cleary Sculpture Garden is a landmark honoring children's book author Beverly Cleary. The garden has statues of the main characters from her books. You will find statues of Ramona Quimby, Henry Huggins, and Henry's dog Ribsy. An artist named Lee Hunt made the statues for the garden. Beverly Cleary was there to see them when the garden opened in 1995.

Directions

In the space below, write your first middle paragraph. The information you filled in on pages 18-19 (under I.) should help you. (Also see pages 15 and 16 for other facts and details.)

First middle paragraph: ....

....

....

....

....

....

....

....

....

Work Zone

Directions Look at the information you filled in on page 19 (under II.) and on pages 15 and 16 to help you write the second middle paragraph.

Second middle paragraph: ....

....

....

....

....

....

....

....

....

....

....

....

....

....

....

Work Zone

Look at the information you filled in on page 19 (under III.) and on pages 15 and 16 to help you write the third middle paragraph.

Third middle paragraph: ....

....

....

....

....

....

....

....

....

....

....

....

....

....

....

....

Date ....

Writing Ending Your Report

My Report

Beginning

Middle

Ending

A good ending sums up information, adds interesting details, or leaves the reader with something to think about. Read the last paragraph of the report on pages 5-6. In it, the writer offers a few more details.

Now read the last paragraph from the report about the Beverly Cleary Sculpture Garden for Children:

The Beverly Cleary Sculpture Garden for Children is one of the few American landmarks to honor an author of children's books. If you ever get to Portland, Oregon, be sure to visit it. In the meantime, you can visit Ramona by reading Mrs. Cleary's wonderful books.

Directions

Use the space below to write the last paragraph of your report. Review the facts you wrote on page 17. Think about how you could use one of those facts in your ending.

Work Zone

....

....

....

....

....

....

....

NEXT STEP

On your own paper, write a neat copy of your whole report. This copy is called a "first draft." It's your first try at writing the entire report. Store it in the back pocket of this booklet.

Revising
Improving Your Writing

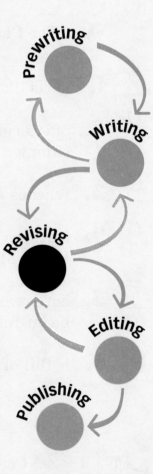

Prewriting

Writing

Revising

Editing

Publishing

Revising Reviewing Topic Sentences

Each of your paragraphs should begin with a topic sentence. A well-written topic sentence does two things: (1) it names the subject of the paragraph and (2) it tells the main idea you are going to focus on. Details (facts, examples, and powerful words) will give the reader more information about your main idea.

Sample Topic Sentence:

The Empire State Building	is one of the tallest buildings in the United States.
(subject)	+ (the main idea)

Work Zone

Directions Match each subject with its main idea. Write the correct letter on the lines below.

A. Glacier National Park   **D.** The Illinois Railway Museum

B. The Gateway Arch   **E.** The Petrified Forest

C. The Seattle Space Needle   **F.** The Painted Desert

___B___ **1.** looks like a giant arch and is called the "Gateway to the West."

___D___ **2.** offers rides on steam, diesel, and electric trains throughout the summer.

___C___ **3.** reaches to the sky and stands for dreams of space flight.

___A___ **4.** features huge glaciers, or ice sheets, that are still carving the Rocky Mountains.

___F___ **5.** isn't really painted, but its rock formations are colorful and beautiful.

___E___ **6.** is full of trees that have turned to stone.

Check the paragraphs in your report to be sure they have clear, specific topic sentences. Rewrite any that are weak or add a topic sentence if one is missing.

Date..............................

Revising Using Transitions Between Paragraphs

Each of your paragraphs includes information about one main idea in your report. To connect those main ideas, use transition words or phrases. They make your report clearer and easier to read.

One paragraph might end this way:

Today the pipeline moves 13 percent of this nation's oil production.

The next paragraph could begin with a transition word:

_____**However**_____ the idea of an 800-mile pipeline seemed impossible in 1968 when oil was discovered in Prudhoe Bay, Alaska.

Directions | Read the rest of that paragraph below. Then choose from the list one transition word or phrase to begin each of the next two paragraphs.

| Soon | After | Even though | Finally | As a result |

Because of three mountain ranges and hundreds of rivers and streams, the engineers had lots of problems to solve. They would need 11 pumping stations to keep the oil moving. Frozen ground meant that all of the pipe would have to be aboveground.

_____**After**_____ all the planning, construction began in the spring of 1975 and ended about two years later. More than 70,000 workers designed and built the $8 billion pipeline. The pipe is four feet across, and its walls are half-inch thick steel.

_____**Even though**_____ the pipe is that big, the oil travels only five and a half miles per hour. It takes about six days for it to reach the port city of Valdez. Every month, about 50 tanker ships are each loaded with 53 million gallons of oil. Seven huge oil companies work together to keep the pipeline pumping oil.

Review your report. Try to use transition words or phrases to connect your paragraphs.

Work Zone

Revising Getting a Second Opinion

Your teacher may want you and a classmate to evaluate each other's writing by completing the sheet below.

Second Opinion

Writer's name: ....   Partner's name: ....

Topic: ....

I think your topic was . . . .

- really interesting to read about.
- full of unusual facts.

I didn't know that . . . .

- some people didn't want the landmark in their town.
- construction was stopped for seven years.

I would like to know more about . . . .

- how the construction crews worked on the mountain.
- how money was raised to pay for the landmark.
- the best time of year to visit the park.

Some favorite words, sentences, and ideas: ....

- the mountain looks right back
- the giants of history
- silence surrounds their faces

Date ....

Revising | Revising in Action

Revising means changing parts of your first draft to make it better. You can make the changes right on the first draft, as in the example below.

A powerful verb shows action.

An idea is made clearer.

A long sentence is changed into two sentences.

> shoots
> What ~~sends~~ a tower of water and steam into the air
> ∧many times a day? If you guessed Old Faithful, you are right͏͏. ~~because~~ Old Faithful is a geyser in Yellowstone National Park in Wyoming. It is one of the most famous landmarks in the United States.

Directions

Read the next part of this research report. Then cross out one unnecessary sentence and combine the underlined sentences. (Write your combined sentence on the lines below.)

> An underground river supplies the water for Old Faithful. ~~I've seen it erupt twice!~~ The water flows over hot rocks deep inside the earth. <u>The water boils there. The heat causes pressure.</u>

The water boils there, and the heat

causes pressure.

_____

Check the sentences in your report. Do any need to be made clearer? Can any short sentences be combined?

Work Zone

Date ....

Revising Checking Your Progress

Directions Check "yes" or "no" for each question below. Then make the needed changes in your report.

Work Zone

YES   NO

Did I FOLLOW a writing plan?

◯ ◯   Did I choose a landmark that I think is interesting?

◯ ◯   Did I find information to answer my questions? (pages 14-16)

◯ ◯   Did I find other interesting facts for my report? (page 17)

Do I need to ADD information?

◯ ◯   Did I write about one main idea (a landmark)?

◯ ◯   Did I include the most important and interesting facts?

Do I need to CUT any information?

◯ ◯   Did I avoid using too many words?

◯ ◯   Did I take out any unnecessary information?

Do I need to REWRITE some parts?

◯ ◯   Does my beginning name the subject and get the reader's attention?

◯ ◯   Do my middle paragraphs share enough important information?

◯ ◯   Does my ending leave the reader with something to think about?

Do I need to REORDER any parts?

◯ ◯   Did I write paragraphs that are easy to follow?

◯ ◯   Did I write a clear beginning, middle, and ending?

Date ....

Revising Adding a Title

Since the title is the first thing that a reader sees, it should be especially interesting. Here are some tips for writing titles.

Title Tips

 Be imaginative.
Ramona Rules in Portland, *not* The Beverly Cleary Sculpture Garden
A Grand Old Geyser, *not* Old Faithful

 Use strong, colorful words.
The Long, Black Wall of Names, *not* The Vietnam Veterans Memorial
A Bird's-Eye View of the Big Apple, *not* New York City Skyscraper

3 Give the words rhythm.
A Sidewalk Scattered with Stars, *not* A Hollywood Sidewalk

Work Zone

Directions Match the creative titles on the right with the names of well-known American landmarks. Write a letter on each line.

_c_ **1.** The Grand Canyon

_d_ **2.** The Statue of Liberty

_a_ **3.** The White House

_b_ **4.** Mount Rushmore

a. Our President's Mansion

b. Peak Personalities

c. An Enormous Gully

d. One Peaceful Lady

Directions Make up titles for the following landmarks.

1. Liberty Bell ....

2. Niagara Falls ....

Compare titles with a partner. Then make up a title for your report.

My title: ....

Revising | Writing a Complete Revised Draft

Directions

Now make all your changes and write a revised copy of your report on your own paper. Then put it in the back pocket of this booklet. Check out the tips below before you start.

On Your Own Paper

Revising Tips

1 Write on every other line and on only one side of the paper. Double-spacing will make editing much easier. (If you use a computer, double-space between lines.)

2 Keep your writing as neat as possible, but don't worry if you cross out a few words.

3 Focus on ideas that need to be changed. Add details, take out words, change the order of some ideas, and rewrite parts wherever you need to.

4 Take your time. You can't make the best changes all at once.

5 Don't get discouraged. You may need to change parts more than once to get them to sound just right. That's okay. It's exactly what professional authors do every day.

6 Save your first draft and your revised draft. Then you will have a record of the changes you have made.

Editing
Checking for Style and Correctness

Prewriting

Writing

Revising

Editing

Publishing

Editing for Style

Making Sentence Beginnings Different

Your writing will sound boring if too many sentences start the same way. Be sure to begin your sentences with different words.

Uninteresting writing:

The workers began blasting on March 17, 1930. The workers worked day and night. The workers took one year and 45 days to finish the tunnel.

Interesting writing:

The construction workers began blasting on March 17, 1930. They worked day and night. One year and 45 days later, the workers had finished the tunnel. (The writer used an adjective, a pronoun, and a change in word order to add interest to his writing.)

Directions

Read the paragraph below. Then change the underlined subjects. Use a pronoun, or move the subject to a different place in the sentence. Rewrite your improved paragraph on the lines that follow.

Work Zone

The Statue of Liberty is one of the most famous landmarks in the United States. The Statue of Liberty is located on an island in the New York Harbor. The Statue of Liberty was the first thing immigrants saw when they arrived in this country.

....

....

....

....

....

Read your new sentences. Do they sound more interesting? Now check the sentences in your report. If too many begin the same way, change some of the beginnings.

Date ....

Editing for Correctness

Capitalizing Names of People and Things

Your report will most likely have names of places and people. Be sure to capitalize them correctly.

- **Capitalize all proper nouns and proper adjectives:**

Beverly Cleary	Golden Gate Bridge	Empire State Building
New York skyline	American landmark	Washington Monument

- **Capitalize specific geographical names** *(streets, cities, states, important regions, countries, land formations, bodies of water):*

Canada	New Mexico	Atlantic Ocean
the Pacific Northwest	Dade County	Route 66
Chicago	Lake Mills	Rocky Mountains

- **Capitalize the names of historical events:**

Civil War	American Revolution	Boston Tea Party

Directions Read each sentence. Then draw three lines under each letter that needs to be capitalized. Write the capital letter above the lowercase one. The number at the end of each sentence tells how many capitals are needed.

Work Zone

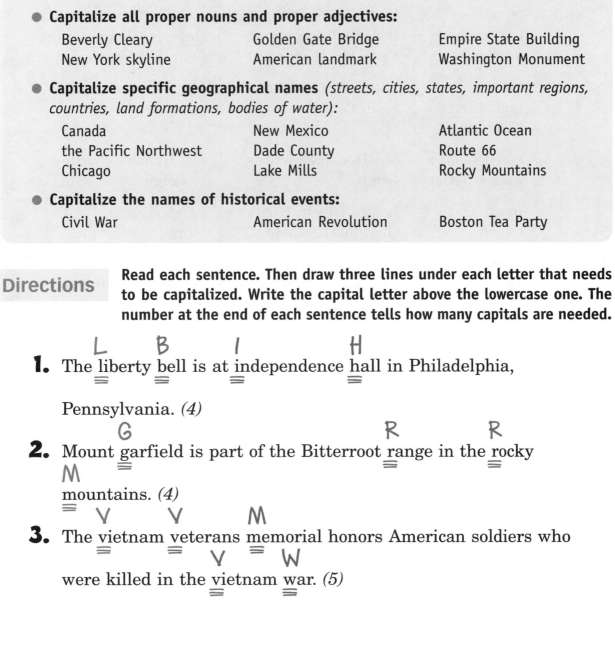

1. The liberty bell is at independence hall in Philadelphia, Pennsylvania. *(4)*

2. Mount garfield is part of the Bitterroot range in the rocky mountains. *(4)*

3. The vietnam veterans memorial honors American soldiers who were killed in the vietnam war. *(5)*

Review your corrected sentences with a classmate. Then check your report to see if you have capitalized words correctly.

Editing Editing and Proofreading Symbols

Use the symbols below when you edit your work. They can help you mark punctuation, spelling, and capitalization changes.

Editing and Proofreading Symbols

Symbol	Meaning	Example	Corrected Example
≡	Capitalize a letter.	Beverly Cleary wrote *Dear Mr. henshaw.*	Beverly Cleary wrote *Dear Mr. Henshaw.*
/	Make a capital letter lowercase.	Leigh Botts is the main Character.	Leigh Botts is the main character.
∧	Insert (add) a word or letter.	Mr. Henshaw writes Leigh.	Mr. Henshaw writes to Leigh.
⌄	Insert a comma.	Leigh lives in Pacific Grove California.	Leigh lives in Pacific Grove, California.
⌄ ⌄⌄ ⌄	Insert an apostrophe or quotation marks.	Leigh has been Mr. Henshaws number one fan since second grade.	Leigh has been Mr. Henshaw's number one fan since second grade.
? ! ∧ ∧	Insert a question mark or an exclamation point.	What problem does Leigh solve? He finds out who was taking his food.	What problem does Leigh solve? He finds out who was taking his food.
⊙	Insert a period.	Leigh writes to Mr. Henshaw He likes his books.	Leigh writes to Mr. Henshaw. He likes his books.
sp.	Correct the spelling error.	Leigh has trubbles in school.	Leigh has troubles in school.
ꝺ	Delete (take out).	Leigh he wants to be an author.	Leigh wants to be an author.
¶	Start a new paragraph.	Leigh receives a postcard from Mr. Henshaw. One day his dad . . .	Leigh receives a postcard from Mr. Henshaw. One day his dad . . .

Date ....

Editing Editing in Action

In the example below, see how symbols are used to edit, or correct, common mistakes.

A verb is changed to agree with the subject.

A spelling error is fixed.

A capital letter is lowercased.

Visitors like to see Old Faithful. Park

rangers predict when it will go off so people

know,
~~knows~~ when to watch. Some people watch Old

benches sp.
Faithful from (benchs). They are about 300

g
feet from the Ǥeyser, so the hot water

does not injure the visitors.

Directions

Edit the next part of the report. Add a comma, capitalize one word, correct a spelling mistake, and change the beginning of the last sentence. (Write the new last sentence on the lines below.)

As people hike near Old Faithful‸they

will find almost a dozen other geysers.

Old Faithful is not the biggest geyser in

yellowstone. Old Faithful is the most
=
though
popular, (tho). sp.

It is the most popular, though.

_____

_____

Work Zone

Date ....

Editing Creating a Bibliography

On page 13, you learned how to record sources for a bibliography. Now you will learn how to put them all together.

A bibliography

- lists sources alphabetically by the author's last name (if given), or by the title name.
- is placed at the end of your report.
- is double-spaced.

Sample Bibliography

Here is a sample bibliography using the sources listed on page 13.

BIBLIOGRAPHY

Carter, James. Personal interview. 12 Dec. 2003.

Dallas, George M. The White House. New York: Famous Homes Press, 1995.

Hayek, Susan. "Welcome Home, Mr. President." American Life 2 May 2000: 8-9.

"Life in the White House." Welcome to the White House. <http://

whitehouse.gov>.

"White House." The World Book Encyclopedia. 2002 ed.

On your own paper, write a bibliography for your report. Include the sources that you listed on your note cards. Remember to put them in alphabetical order as shown above. Store your paper in the back pocket of this booklet.

Date ....

Work Zone

Editing & Proofreading Checking Your Progress

Directions Check "yes" or "no" for each of the questions below. Then make corrections in your report until all the answers are "yes."

✳ It's very easy to miss errors when you edit and proofread your own writing, so ask a teacher or a classmate for help.

YES NO

Sentence Structure

○ ○ Did I write clear, complete sentences?

○ ○ Did I vary my sentence beginnings? (See page 36.)

Punctuation

○ ○ Did I end each sentence with the correct punctuation?

○ ○ Did I use commas correctly?

Capitalization

○ ○ Did I start all of my sentences with capital letters?

○ ○ Did I capitalize the names of specific people and places? (See page 37.)

Grammar

○ ○ Did I use the correct form of verbs *(give, gave, given)*?

○ ○ Did I make sure my subjects and verbs agree?
(Paula laughs. Snakes slither.)

Usage

○ ○ Did I use specific nouns and vivid verbs in my writing?

○ ○ Did I use the correct word *(they're, there,* or *their)*?

Spelling

○ ○ Did I check for spelling errors?

○ ○ Did I use a dictionary or a computer spell checker?

On the Next Page

Writing the Final Copy

Directions
You've come to the last step! It's time to write a final copy of your report on pages 43-46. Proofread your report carefully before you hand it in. Save your first draft, revised draft, and the final copy in the back pocket of this booklet. Keep the following tips in mind as you write.

Tips for Handwritten Final Copies

- Use your best penmanship.
- Write in blue or black ink.
- Write your name, your teacher's name, the class, and the date in the upper left-hand corner of page 1.
- Center the title on the first line.
- Skip a line, and start your writing. (This has already been done for you.)
- Indent the first line of each new paragraph.
- Leave a one-inch margin around each page.
- Write your last name and the page number in the upper right-hand corner of every page after page 1.

Jones 2

Tyisha Jones
Mr. Alexander
Language Arts
October 6, 2003

A Grand Old Geyser

What shoots a tower of water and steam into the air many times a day? If you guessed Old Faithful, you are right. Old Faithful is a geyser in Yellowstone National Park in Wyoming. It is one of the most famous landmarks in the United States.

An underground river supplies the water for Old Faithful. The water flows over hot rocks deep inside the earth. It boils there, and the heat causes pressure. Whoosh, a tower of hot water and steam can blast as high as 180 feet into the air.

Visitors like to see Old Faithful. Park rangers predict when it will go off so people know when to watch. Some

Research Reports **43**

Tips for Computer Copies

- Use an easy-to-read font and a 10- or 12-point type size.
- Double-space throughout your writing.
- Leave a one-inch margin around each page.